HOW TO SEE
IN THE
SPIRIT

EXERCISES &
ACTIVATIONS

MICHAEL VAN VLYMEN

ISBN: 978-1-948680-91-2

CONTENTS

INTRODUCTION

Welcome to a journey of spiritual growth, activation, and discovery. This book is not about seeking spiritual "thrills" or chasing supernatural experiences for their own sake. That can be pointless at best and dangerous at worst. Instead, it is about equipping and training you to walk more powerfully in the call that God has placed on your life. It's about developing the spiritual tools and sensitivity you need to fulfill your destiny, deepen your relationship with the Lord, and impact the world for His kingdom.

Why This Book Matters

As believers, we are called to live a life led by the Spirit. The Bible is filled with examples of people who walked in close partnership with God, operating in spiritual gifts, hearing His voice, and moving in His power. From Moses at the burning bush to Isaiah in the throne room, from Peter stepping out of the boat to Paul receiving visions, the spiritual realm has always been integral to God's plans for His people. These were not extraordinary moments reserved for a select few—they were examples of what is possible for all believers who are willing to pursue God wholeheartedly.

This book is designed to help you step into that same spiritual reality, not through abstract teaching and strange convoluted instructions, but through practical exercises and activations that engage your faith and awaken your spiritual senses. Each exercise is rooted in biblical principles, intended to guide you into deeper intimacy with God while training you to see, hear, and move in the Spirit. These are things I do or have done in my own walk with God.

The Purpose of Spiritual Exercises

The exercises in this book are not simply about learning how to "do" things in the spiritual realm; they are about transformation—becoming someone fully aligned with God's purposes and walking in the fullness of His calling. These activations are far more than techniques or rituals; they are opportunities to shape your character, deepen your faith, and strengthen your spiritual awareness.

Each exercise is designed to stretch your faith, inviting you to step into the unseen and trust God more deeply. Faith, after all, is the foundation of all spiritual growth, and these practices encourage you to rely on His presence and guidance even when things feel unfamiliar. These are not abstract or empty routines but moments of encounter, opportunities to draw closer to God's heart and sense His nearness in profound ways.

At the same time, these exercises serve as training for the unique calling God has placed on your life. Every believer has a purpose, and fulfilling that purpose requires spiritual maturity and sensitivity. Through these activations, you are equipping yourself to hear His voice more clearly, discern His will more accurately, and respond to His leading with confidence. They have a purpose.

As you engage with these practices, you are also preparing yourself for spiritual impact. God has called each of us to serve His kingdom, and the more trained and equipped we are, the more effectively we can carry out His work. This is not a journey of self-improvement or spiritual experimentation; it is a pathway to becoming the person God created you to be—empowered, prepared, and ready to partner closely with Him in extraordinary ways.

How to Approach This Journey

Spiritual growth, like any meaningful endeavor, requires commitment and discipline. These exercises are not something you try once, but practices that gain depth and power through regular engagement. Think of them as spiritual workouts. Just as physical exercise strengthens your body over time, these activations will strengthen your spiritual senses and build your capacity to operate in the spiritual realm. Set aside intentional time to engage fully with each exercise, approaching it with focus and expectation.

As you start on this journey, keep your Bible close and your heart grounded in truth. The spiritual realm is vast and complex, and discernment is essential. Always measure your experiences and insights against the Word of God. Scripture is your plumbline, your safeguard, and your guide, ensuring that what you receive aligns with His character and purposes. Be diligent in seeking His truth, and allow the Holy Spirit to confirm what is from Him.

While vigilance is necessary, there is no need to approach this journey with fear. God has not given us a spirit of fear but of power, love, and a sound mind. Trust that He is with you every step of the way, guiding and protecting you as you explore deeper dimensions of faith. Step out in boldness, knowing that your desire to draw closer to Him honors Him and delights His heart.

Above all, pursue this journey with *passion*. God invites us to seek Him with all our heart, soul, mind, and strength, holding nothing back. Let your hunger for His presence and your desire to grow in Him drive you forward, even when the process feels challenging. Spiritual growth is rarely easy, but it is always worth it. Every step you take brings you closer to Him, equips you more fully for His purposes, and opens the door to a life that is rich in faith, power, and intimacy with the One who calls you His own.

What to Expect in This Book

This book is primarily focused on exercises and activations, not extensive teaching. The purpose is not to repeat material you may have read in my previous books or elsewhere, but to provide practical tools for putting what you know into action. However, for clarity, each activation includes a brief explanation of its purpose and foundation in Scripture.

Expect to engage your imagination, your senses, and your faith in new ways. God has given us powerful tools, such as stillness, silence, and imagination, to connect with Him and the spiritual realm. These exercises will help you sharpen those tools, making you more attuned to His voice and His movements.

Why You Should Do This

The spiritual realm is real, and as believers, we are called to navigate it wisely. These exercises are not about escaping into fantasy but about training yourself to perceive and operate in the unseen with maturity and confidence.

Consider Jesus' words: *"Very truly I tell you, whoever believes in me will do the works I have been doing, and they will do even greater things than these, because I am going to the Father"* (John 14:12). This is the life we are invited into—not a passive faith, but an active, powerful partnership with God.

A Final Word of Encouragement

God sees your heart. He knows the desires of your heart and your desire to grow closer to Him. He is faithful to meet you as you step out in faith. Each exercise in this book is a prayer in motion, an act of faith that invites His presence and His work in your life.

You may feel unsure or awkward at first, but don't let that discourage you. Like any skill, spiritual sensitivity develops with practice. Be patient with yourself, have some grace for yourself, trust the process, and lean into the guidance of the Holy Spirit.

This journey is not just about learning some new things— it's about transformation. God is preparing you for greater things. He is equipping you to walk boldly in your calling, to hear His voice clearly, and to move powerfully in His Spirit. Let this book be a guide to you as you take those steps of faith.

Let's begin.

CHAPTER ONE

SPIRITUAL SIGHT

Sight Through Intentional Looking

It's really my heart to help people understand what's really happening as they seek to see or begin to see in the spiritual realm. What are we seeing? What realm are we seeing? Are we seeing with our natural eyes or our spiritual eyes? That's really not even the tip of the iceberg. Things are not always what they appear and that's ok. The more time we spend in that world or that realm, the easier it becomes to make these distinctions. I would say going forward that it's all going to work out. Just remember to keep the Word of God as your plumbline and declare the blood of Jesus over your quest. And if you're going to do it, do it.

Spiritual sight is not bound by the limitations of physical sight. While our physical eyes allow us to see the tangible, material world, our spiritual eyes open a window to the unseen realm. This realm is filled with God's presence, angelic activity, and many things we won't necessarily understand, especially at first Yet, for many, if not most, accessing spiritual sight can feel elusive or even impossible. Developing this ability requires us to look with intention, an intentional "seeing" or an intentional *desire* to see that gradually awakens our spiritual eyes. I say gradually because the process is like exercise, like building a muscle through regular use. The more you practice the more you see and understand.

This process of engaging spiritual sight requires patience, faith, and practice. By intentionally focusing on what we cannot see in the physical—looking with both open and closed eyes—we signal to our spirit and inform our soul that we are ready and willing to perceive. Over time this practice brings about a shift: our spirit begins to "see" in ways that our physical senses cannot, and we start to discern and see, hear, feel and know, spiritual realities around us. Let's look deeper into this process, exploring how and why intentional looking activates spiritual sight.

Looking with Eyes Open

Looking with physical eyes open is often where we start when we desire to see spiritually. We might be aware that there is more to see around us than the physical, but we are not yet fully attuned to the spiritual realm. There are many ways we can intentionally engage our spiritual sight with open eyes:

Choosing to Focus with Intention

Begin by gazing softly around the space you're in, Why do I say "gazing softly"? I say it because striving for this at any level is harmful to the process. "I'm trying hard to see" is not something helpful. Focusing with intention must be done in a restful, relaxed manner. You are not looking for anything specific but rather opening yourself to a new way of seeing. Instead of focusing on physical things, allow your focus to soften, as though you are looking *through* the physical environment. Pray a simple prayer like, "Lord, help me see what is unseen. Open my spiritual eyes."

Sensing Beyond the Physical

As you look, become aware that there is more happening in the room than what is visible to the natural eye. Realize and acknowledge that the spiritual realm is active, that God's presence is near, and that the atmosphere is filled with spiritual realities, even if they are invisible. This awareness signals to your spirit to be attentive.

Inviting Perception

Sometimes you may sense a slight shift, a warmth, or a gentle impression in your spirit as you look with intention. This can be an indicator that you are beginning to see spiritually. At that point it is important to not get excited. Getting excited or fearful or any other strong emotion will close that awareness very quickly. Why? Because the sudden focus on the physical closes down the spiritual. It doesn't always stay that way but it definitely starts that way. We have to cultivate the normalcy of being in the spirit. Stay in a relaxed state and with time and practice, you will notice faint impressions, subtle changes in light, or a sense of presence that grows stronger.

Looking with open eyes focuses your intention on the unseen realm, allowing your spirit to gradually "tune in." This process of intentional seeing develops a new layer of awareness. Even though our eyes may not visibly see into the spirit realm immediately, this act of intentionality primes our spiritual senses, inviting the Holy Spirit to awaken our sight.

Looking with Eyes Closed

When we close our eyes, we block out physical distractions, allowing us to concentrate more deeply on spiritual impressions. In this practice, looking becomes less about what we see with our physical vision and more about what we perceive with our spirit. Even though it may feel like we are still looking with our physical eyes even with them closed. It is what we are familiar with. Here's how to engage in this focused seeing with eyes closed:

Setting the Intention

Begin by closing your eyes and setting your intention to perceive what God may reveal. Remind yourself that just because your physical eyes are closed does not mean you cannot see; instead, you are opening the "eyes of your heart" (Ephesians 1:18) to see what God is showing.

Looking into the "Empty" Space

With your eyes closed, visualize yourself looking into the space around you. Acknowledge that the space is not truly empty but filled with God's presence, spiritual activity, and angels etc... Hold the intention to see without focusing on anything but rather looking to see if you can indeed see anything spiritual. In your intention you are allowing your spirit to engage and become active.

Waiting and Allowing the Shift

As you continue looking with intention, you may start to sense a shift in your awareness. This shift is subtle; it might feel like a lightening of the mind, a softening, or a sense of anticipation. It can often be a lack of awareness of your physical self and an "awakening" of your spirit. This shift signals that your spiritual eyes are beginning to engage, moving beyond physical sight into spiritual perception. I say perception because there are many ways to see but the reality is that your spiritual eyes truly see.

Recognizing Impressions

In this state, you may begin to see impressions—shapes, colors, light, or even images that come before your eyes. These impressions or visions, are not seen with physical eyes but with the eyes of your spirit. Trust that even the faintest impression is a step toward clearer spiritual sight. Acknowledge these impressions, allowing them to unfold naturally without questioning or analyzing.

Closing your eyes removes the distractions of the physical world, making it easier for your spirit to engage. When we look with intention, fully aware that the "empty" space around us is filled with a real and solid spiritual presence, our spirit begins to shift from physical sight to spiritual sight. This process gradually awakens our spiritual vision, allowing us to perceive subtle impressions and insights.

Why This Practice Awakens Spiritual Sight

The practice of looking with intention—whether with eyes open or closed—awakens spiritual sight because it focuses our mind and spirit on what is unseen, inviting God's presence to reveal Himself. I'm sure you have heard the spiritual maxim the what you focus on you will connect with. By repeatedly looking without expecting immediate physical results, we are training ourselves to see, recognize and interpret spiritual impressions. This discipline builds a bridge between our natural and spiritual senses, helping us perceive the things of the spirit and spiritual activity. It is in these processes that we begin to cultivate awareness of the spiritual realm.

Over time, a process of "spiritual synesthesia" occurs: we become able to see spiritual realities in ways that combine multiple senses. For instance, we may see a glow of light while feeling a sense of peace, or "hear" an impression in our mind while sensing warmth in our heart. This multisensory integration enriches our perception, grounding our spirit in an understanding that God is always actively present in our lives. He isn't far away, He is right there with us.

This practice is based on faith and commitment. When we practice looking with intention, we express faith that God will meet us in our seeking, fulfilling His promise to reveal Himself to those who earnestly seek Him. We believe Him therefore we act on His promises. As Jesus said, *"Blessed are the pure in heart, for they will see God"* (Matthew 5:8). Our pursuit of spiritual sight is ultimately a pursuit of God Himself, growing in love and closeness to Him.

Embracing the Process of Awakening

As you engage in these practices regularly, remember that spiritual sight may develop gradually. Some days, you may sense more vividly, while other days may feel quiet or even empty. The reasons are many. One day you may be distracted and another day tired. One day you are overwhelmed with a busy mind, another day you forget all about what you are doing. Trust that each moment of intentional seeing brings growth, even if it seems subtle at first. Our spirit man sees with great clarity and we are in the process of creating a conscious awareness of what our spirit sees and discerns. It is a melding of communication amongst our being. We learn through repeated practice, and over time, spiritual sight grows sharper, clearer, and more responsive.

This journey of spiritual sight is about more than just seeing the unseen; it is about connecting with God's heart, perceiving His movement, and aligning our lives with His will in our lives. The more we engage, the more we'll find ourselves able to navigate the spiritual realm with confidence, guided by the light of His presence, the direction of the Holy Spirit and the vision of His truth.

INTENTIONAL LOOKING EXERCISES

Here are three simple, yet effective, intentional looking exercises designed to open and sharpen your spiritual sight. These exercises focus on being fully present and engaged with both the physical and spiritual realms, helping to train your spiritual senses while relying on the Holy Spirit to lead in the process.

1. FOCUS ON THE EMPTY SPACE

Train your eyes and spirit to perceive the invisible through intentional stillness and observation.

Choose a quiet, dimly lit room where you won't be disturbed. Sit comfortably and pray: "Lord, open my eyes to see what You want me to see. Help me perceive the unseen with clarity and discernment."

Focus your physical eyes on an "empty" area of the room, such as the middle area, a doorway, or a blank wall. Keep your gaze soft and relaxed, looking at the open areas where no furniture is placed, in effect, examining the air or the space of the room.

Be still and attentive to what you sense. Do you notice subtle changes, such as flickers of light, faint movements, or atmospheric shifts? Pay attention to any inner impressions or feelings as well.

If you notice anything, ask the Lord: "What does this mean? Is there something You want me to understand?" Trust the Holy Spirit to bring clarity.

After 10–15 minutes, write down what you observed or felt. Repeat this exercise daily, and you'll begin to notice an increase in your spiritual perception.

2. Details of Creation" Exercise

Use physical objects to train your spirit to see God's handiwork and recognize His presence through intentional observation.

Choose an object from nature, such as a flower, leaf, or stone, and place it in front of you. Pray: "Holy Spirit, help me see beyond the surface. Reveal to me Your glory in creation."

Look closely at the object, examining every detail—the texture, shape, colors, and patterns. Notice the intricacies and ask yourself questions like: What does this reveal about God's creativity and care?

Shift your focus from the physical characteristics to what the object might symbolize spiritually. For example, a flower might remind you of God's provision (Matthew 6:28), or a stone might symbolize strength and stability.

Speak to God as you observe, asking Him to show you deeper truths. Write down any impressions, scriptures, or revelations that come to mind.

Repeat this exercise with different objects in various environments (e.g., a tree, a body of water, or the sky). Over time, you'll develop a heightened ability to "see" God's presence in the physical and spiritual realms.

3. THE "SEEING IN STILLNESS" EXERCISE

Combine physical stillness with spiritual openness to enhance your ability to perceive spiritual realities.

Sit in a comfortable position, either indoors or outdoors, where you can relax and be undisturbed. Begin with a prayer: "Lord, as I sit still before You, open my spiritual eyes. Let me see beyond the natural and discern Your presence."

Close your eyes and take a few deep breaths, allowing yourself to relax fully. Open your eyes softly and focus on a fixed point in the room or environment, such as a distant tree, a candle flame, or a shadowed corner.

Without moving your gaze, become aware of your peripheral vision. Notice any changes in light, movement, or atmospheric shifts. Pay attention to what you see "out of the corner of your eye."

Ask God to reveal what you're observing spiritually. For example, if you notice a flicker of light, ask: "Lord, is this Your presence, or is there something You want me to understand?"

Continue the exercise for 10–15 minutes, allowing yourself to relax further into the process. The more you practice, the more likely you are to experience subtle spiritual impressions or sights.

Journal your observations after each session, noting any patterns or revelations over time. This practice helps train your spiritual eyes while fostering a deeper connection with God.

Encouragement

These intentional looking exercises are not just about "seeing" in the physical sense. They are opportunities to begin to train yourself to cooperate with your spirit in recognizing God's presence and activity. Be patient with yourself as you practice, and trust that the Holy Spirit is sharpening your spiritual sight, even if the results feel subtle at first. Over time, your perception will deepen, and you'll grow in confidence as you learn to discern what God is showing you.

CHAPTER TWO

SEEING WITH CLOSED EYES

A Gateway to Spiritual Sight

Many people believe that if their eyes are closed, they cannot see. While this is mostly true for physical sight, it doesn't apply to spiritual sight. In the unseen realm, seeing with closed eyes is entirely possible, though it requires practice, patience, and intentional focus. The spirit has its own way of perceiving, and by learning to look with closed eyes, we open ourselves to subtle shifts, colors, and movements that hint at spiritual realities. This practice is like adjusting to dim light or learning to notice fine details in the dark.

Just as our eyes adjust to physical darkness over time, our spiritual eyes adjust as we patiently look into the unseen. With intention, we begin to perceive faint impressions and gentle shifts, each one guiding us deeper into spiritual awareness.

Understanding "Seeing" with Closed Eyes

When you close your eyes, your physical sight is limited, but not entirely absent. For instance, if you close your eyes in a bright room, you can still sense light and darkness. By moving your hand in front of your closed eyes, you can observe a faint shift in the darkness as your hand blocks out the light. This simple experiment demonstrates that even with closed eyes, we can still perceive.

In the same way, when we turn our attention to the spirit and look with our eyes closed, our spiritual vision, though initially subtle, can begin to reveal impressions that go beyond physical sight. The process of looking without seeing physical objects helps us shift from natural seeing to spiritual seeing, training ourselves to detect impressions, colors, or movements that reveal the presence and activity of the spiritual realm. This type of sight may start faintly but becomes clearer over time as we practice and acknowledge the impressions we receive.

Practical Steps for Developing Spiritual Sight with Closed Eyes

Begin with a Quiet, Intentional Focus

Find a quiet place to sit comfortably, (like a prayer chair) close your eyes, and take a few deep breaths. Pray a simple prayer like, "Lord, help me to see with my spiritual eyes. Open my vision to perceive what You are doing around me."

Set your intention to look, even though your physical eyes are closed. Think of it as being in a very dark room yet looking because you know that eventually your eyes will adjust to the dark. You are aware that there is much to see, though you may see little at first.

Observe the Subtle Shifts

As you sit with eyes closed, imagine a dim light filling the room around you. Without focusing on anything specific, allow your awareness to rest in this dimness, observing any changes you might sense. Just as when you're looking into low light, your mind might initially only perceive vague impressions.

After a few moments, you may start to notice faint shifts or movements in the "atmosphere" around you. This could feel like a gentle breeze, a sense of warmth or coolness, or a slight darkening and lightening in your field of perception. What I have observed mostly at first were waves in the atmosphere bending and moving like heat rising from a blacktop road on a hot summer day. The atmosphere itself can begin to move and bend or vibrate. Acknowledge these sensations as the beginnings of spiritual sight, knowing that God is opening your vision.

It may sound as if I am repeating myself because I am. This is not rocket science, they are simple and direct exercises that we can do that bring awareness and help facilitate the opening of our spiritual eyes and a conscious awareness of the spiritual realm.

Look for Faint Colors and Light

With continued focus, you may begin to notice faint colors—like soft hues of blue, purple, or gold—moving near and then drifting away. These colors may be subtle and even fleeting, but they represent spiritual activity, symbolic impressions, angels or God's presence drawing near.

Pay attention to these colors without forcing them or trying to hold onto them. Allow yourself to see these impressions as a natural part of your spiritual sight, simply *observing* what unfolds. Over time, these colors may become more vivid or take on specific meanings, helping you interpret what God is revealing. Often you are only seeing a piece of something that will unfold as you pay attention.

Wait with Patience and Expectation

The key to developing spiritual sight with closed eyes is patience. This is not a practice of immediate results; it's a gradual adjustment to seeing with your spirit and having a conscious awareness of it. Are you willing to put in the time? Is it worth it to you? By waiting with expectation, you signal to your spirit that you're ready to receive.

Sit quietly, trusting that each time you look with intention, you're strengthening your spiritual sight whether you are seeing anything substantive or not. Like adjusting to low light, the more you practice, the more your spirit "sees." Over time, you may even begin to perceive subtle movements that signify spiritual presence—angelic beings, God's light, or a shift in atmosphere that points to some type of spiritual communication.

The Growth Process

The journey of seeing with closed eyes is one of growth, where subtle impressions eventually give way to clearer vision. At first, you may only see faint shifts or impressions, but over time, you learn to recognize these subtleties as real. This shift in perception is a process of gradually expanding awareness, one that deepens with faithful practice. Here's how this growth occurs:

At the beginning, you might see faint glows, soft colors, or vague shifts in the darkness. These impressions may feel insignificant, but they are indeed foundational to developing spiritual sight. Each time you practice, you're teaching yourself to recognize and respond to these impressions.

Understanding that what you see is real: As you continue, you'll become more confident that these subtle impressions are truly spiritual. Recognize them as glimpses of spiritual activity, and celebrate each small sign as a step forward.

Awareness Expands with Focused Observation: Over time, you may find that these impressions "expand" as you look with *relaxed attention*. This is similar to noticing fine details in a dimly lit room—our perception adjusts, and we see more as we focus and become accustomed to the spiritual atmosphere. With each practice, your awareness grows, allowing you to see with greater clarity.

Night Practice: Looking with Open Eyes in Low Light

A related practice to seeing with closed eyes is looking with open eyes in low light, such as at night while waiting on God or lying in bed. In low light, physical objects lose their detail, allowing us to see with a softer focus. This is similar to seeing spiritually because it requires us to focus beyond what is directly visible.

Soft Gaze in the Dark

While lying in bed or sitting in a dimly lit room, allow your gaze to soften, focusing on the darkness or shadows in the room. You may notice faint shapes, shadows, or movements in the atmosphere. These impressions may be subtle, but they reflect spiritual presence or activity.

Observing with Intention

As you continue looking with a soft gaze, hold the intention to see spiritually. Notice any impressions of light, faint color, or movement in the atmosphere. Allow yourself to "see" with an open, relaxed attention. This is not about seeing physical details but about perceiving the subtle presence of the spiritual.

Expanding Vision through Attention

In the same way that you may see more with closed eyes over time, your vision in low light can expand as you continue looking with intention. You adjust to the subtlety, and your awareness begins to open to spiritual presence. With patience, what starts as faint shadows or soft colors may become clearer, helping you grow more comfortable in the process of seeing in the spirit.

Why This Practice is Valuable

Seeing with closed eyes or in low light teaches us to perceive beyond the limitations of natural sight. Each time we practice, we awaken and strengthen our spiritual vision, training ourselves to recognize what lies before us in the unseen realm. These practices require faith and patience, as well as a trust that God will meet us in our seeking.

By looking intentionally, both with closed eyes and in low light, we grow our awareness of the subtle and gradual. Over time, we find ourselves able to see more clearly, gaining a richer understanding of the spiritual realm that surround us. This process not only expands our vision but also draws us closer to God, whose presence is always near, ready to be revealed to those who are willing to look.

Seeing with Closed Eyes Exercises

Seeing with closed eyes is a powerful way to engage your spiritual sight and imagination. By closing your physical eyes, you reduce distractions and allow yourself to focus on perceiving the unseen realm. Here are three exercises designed to help you sharpen this practice and cultivate greater spiritual vision:

1. The "Inner Room" Exercise

Training your spiritual sight by creating a place in your imagination for encountering God.

First find a quiet place where you can sit comfortably. Close your eyes and pray: "Lord, I invite You into this moment. Help me see with my spiritual eyes and guide me into Your presence."

In your mind, imagine stepping into a beautiful room—a private sanctuary designed just for you and God. Picture the details: the walls, the lighting, the furniture, and the atmosphere.

Visualize Jesus entering the room. How does He look? What does His presence feel like? Notice every detail—the expression on His face, the way He moves, and how you feel in His presence. Utilize all of your senses as you interact with the Lord.

Take a few moments to talk with Jesus or simply sit with Him. Ask Him questions, listen for His responses, or just enjoy being in His presence.

After 10–15 minutes, open your eyes and write down what you saw and experienced. Repeat this exercise regularly, allowing the details and interactions to deepen over time.

2. The "Light of Heaven" Exercise

Focus on perceiving the light of God's presence and the atmosphere of heaven with your spiritual eyes.

Close your eyes and take a few deep breaths, coming into rest. Pray: "Lord, let me see the light of Your presence. Open my spiritual eyes to see the glory of heaven."

Imagine a brilliant light surrounding you—soft yet radiant, warm yet powerful. This light represents the glory of God. Picture it filling the room, surrounding you, and even entering into you.

Pay attention to the qualities of the light. Is it pure white, golden, or shimmering with colors? Does it move or remain still? How does it feel? Is it powerful and alive? Ask God to show you what the light represents or to reveal Himself through it.

Imagine how the light feels—its warmth, its weightlessness, or its energy. What emotions does it stir in you?

After a few minutes, open your eyes and journal about the experience. How did the light make you feel? Did you sense God's presence more clearly? Over time, this exercise helps you recognize God's light in both the spiritual and natural realms.

3. The "Biblical Encounter Reimagined" Exercise

Enter into a biblical scene to experience it personally and connect with God's revelation through spiritual vision.

Choose a vivid passage of Scripture to meditate on. For example, Isaiah's vision of God in the temple (Isaiah 6:1-8) or Jesus calming the storm (Mark 4:35-41). Read the passage slowly and prayerfully.

Close your eyes and place yourself in the story. Imagine the sights, sounds, and smells. What do you see in the atmosphere? Who is present, and what are they doing?

Visualize yourself as a participant in the scene. If you're in Isaiah's vision, imagine standing beside him as he sees God on His throne. If you're in the boat with Jesus, picture the wind and waves before He calms the storm.

Allow yourself to interact with the scene. Speak with Isaiah or the disciples. Ask Jesus questions about what is happening or listen to what He might say to you personally in that moment.

Afterward, write down your impressions and any insights God revealed to you during the exercise. Repeat this with different passages to expand your spiritual sight and deepen your connection to Scripture.

Looking with Closed Eyes Exercises

These exercises are designed to train your spiritual sight by focusing your attention with intentionality and expectation. Each one uses the concept of looking while your physical eyes are closed, sharpening your awareness and creating space for your spiritual eyes to open. These exercises draw from real-world experiences, like being on guard duty or adjusting to a dark room, to engage your imagination and align your senses with the unseen realm.

1. The Vigilant Guard Exercise

This exercise as well as others below are things that I do on a regular basis to set the stage or get things going in the right direction. Why do I keep doing this after all of these years? I do it because it works well for me. Many people get distracted and like to have something to focus on or meditate on to keep their minds from wandering as they wait on God. This exercise keeps you focused and in the direction you need to go.

Train your spiritual awareness by imagining the intense focus and vigilance of a guard on duty. But remember that even in this scenario we are not striving. We remain in an intense *restful* focus.

Sit in a quiet, undisturbed place where you can relax and focus. Close your eyes and take a few deep breaths, allowing yourself to become still. Pray: "Lord, help me to see with the diligence of a watchful guard. Open my spiritual eyes to perceive anything around me and You want to show me."

Imagine yourself standing guard at the entrance to an important place—a fortress, a city gate, or even the door of your own home. You have a vital responsibility to watch for anything approaching, whether friendly or hostile. Picture yourself fully alert, scanning the horizon, ears tuned to the faintest sound.

With your eyes closed, actively "look" into the unseen. Imagine that you can see movements in the distance, faint lights, or approaching figures. Stay focused, as though it's your duty to protect what's behind you. Ask yourself: What do I see? What do I hear?

As impressions or images begin to form, ask the Lord for clarity. "Lord, is this something I should focus on? What are You revealing to me?" Trust the Holy Spirit to guide your observations.

After 10–15 minutes, open your eyes and journal what you saw, felt, or heard. Over time, this exercise will strengthen your ability to stay spiritually vigilant and alert. I use this exercise quite often.

2. THE DARK ROOM ADJUSTMENT EXERCISE

In this exercise you train your spiritual sight by imagining the natural process of your eyes adjusting to darkness and trusting that spiritual sight will emerge with patience and expectation. If we look with our physical eyes and there is nothing physical to see, our spiritual eyes begin to engage.

Close your eyes and take a moment to relax. Pray: "Lord, as my physical eyes are closed, I ask You to open my spiritual eyes. Help me to perceive Your light and any movements in the unseen."

Imagine that you are in a completely dark room. At first, you see nothing but blackness. However, you know that your eyes will adjust to the dark, as they do naturally, allowing you to begin perceiving shapes, shadows, or faint sources of light.

With this awareness, begin to "look" around as if your physical eyes are open. Picture yourself turning your head slowly, scanning the room. Do you notice any faint light or subtle movements? Trust that as you continue to look, your spiritual sight will adjust, just as your physical eyes adjust to low light. The things you see at first can be so faint and so fleeting it can be hard to acknowledge them and accept the progress. Celebrate everything you see no matter how small.

If you sense something—light, a figure, or an impression—ask the Holy Spirit to give you understanding. "Lord, what am I seeing? What do You want me to understand?"

Practice this exercise regularly, and each time, look for small improvements in what you perceive. Write down your observations after each session to track your progress. This exercise teaches patience and trust, both vital for spiritual growth.

3. THE NIGHT WATCH EXERCISE

This exercise is similar to the first in that you train your spiritual awareness by imagining yourself as a watchman keeping vigil through the night.

Close your eyes and sit in a comfortable position. Pray: "Lord, I take my place as a spiritual watchman. Open my eyes to see the things of the Spirit and give me clarity to discern what is before me."

Picture yourself standing at a high vantage point, such as a city wall or a mountain overlook. You could even be the watchman on the wall from Psalm 130:6

I wait for the Lord more than watchmen wait for the morning, more than watchmen wait for the morning.

It is nighttime, and you are on the night watch, responsible for protecting those who rest below. The sky is dark, but you see faint stars above, and the air is filled with stillness.

Begin scanning the horizon with your spiritual eyes, as though you are looking for signs of movement or light. Imagine your eyes adjusting to the darkness, allowing you to perceive more details. Are there faint glimmers of light approaching? Shadows moving in the distance?

As you "see" things in your spiritual vision, ask the Lord for discernment. "Lord, is this something I need to pray about? What are You revealing to me?" Imagine yourself praying for the safety and protection of what lies behind you.

Afterward, write down what you observed or felt during the exercise. This practice sharpens your spiritual vision while also teaching you to intercede as a watchman.

Each of these exercises trains your spirit to see with expectation and focus, even when your physical eyes are closed. Be patient with yourself as you practice, trusting that God is at work, even if the results feel subtle at first. Over time, you'll find that your spiritual sight becomes sharper, your discernment grows, and your confidence in God is doing in your life increases. Remember, your role is to be faithful in looking and seeking—God will open your eyes in His perfect timing.

CHAPTER THREE

PERIPHERAL VISION

I'll never forget the first time I noticed what looked like fire flickering in my peripheral vision during prayer. It was faint at first, a subtle glow on my left side, about three feet away. At first, I ignored it, thinking perhaps it was a trick of my eyes or the lighting in the room. But as I continued to pray, the fire seemed to grow—becoming brighter, more intense, and impossible to dismiss. Naturally, I turned to look directly at it, but when I did, it disappeared entirely. Puzzled, I returned to prayer, and after 10 or 15 minutes, the flickering flame reappeared in my peripheral vision. This pattern repeated for weeks: the fire would appear when I wasn't directly looking, but the moment I tried to focus my physical eyes on it, it vanished.

I shared this experience with a friend, hoping for insight. He listened politely, but his response was far from what I expected. "You might want to get that checked out," he said. "It could be a detached retina—or maybe a brain tumor." I laughed at first, thinking he was joking, but he was serious. He had no grid for understanding this kind of spiritual phenomenon and could only interpret it through a natural lens. I tried to explain what I was experiencing, that it wasn't physical but spiritual, but my words fell on skeptical ears.

Over the following months, I continued to experience this fire during times of prayer. Each time, it seemed to grow in size and intensity, as if responding to the depth of my intercession. It wasn't until much later that I finally encountered the truth behind the flame. One day, while praying, the fire didn't vanish when I turned to look. Instead, it resolved into the figure of an angel whose very appearance was as fire, clothed in flame. The joy of that moment was indescribable. What began as a fleeting glimpse through peripheral vision became a profound and life-changing encounter.

This experience taught me an important lesson about spiritual sight—often, it begins in subtle and unexpected ways. Peripheral vision, in particular, plays a unique role in helping us perceive the spiritual realm. It allows us to see "without looking," bypassing our natural instincts to control or analyze what we see. For me, what started as an unexplained flicker in my peripheral vision became an invitation to grow in spiritual sensitivity. And it is this invitation that I'm excited to share with you as we explore the role of peripheral vision in spiritual sight.

The Role of Peripheral Vision in Spiritual Sight

Many people begin their journey into spiritual sight not by directly perceiving the spiritual realm but through fleeting glimpses caught in their peripheral vision. It might be a flicker of light, the movement of a shadow, or even a faint impression of a figure. These moments are often subtle and brief but unmistakably real. They leave an impression of having seen something beyond the natural.

The challenge arises when we try to "look" at what we've seen by turning our heads or focusing our physical eyes. Often, the spiritual image or movement seems to vanish, leaving us puzzled or even doubting what we experienced. This happens because spiritual sight operates differently from physical sight. When we turn to look with our physical eyes, we are relying on natural senses to perceive something that is inherently spiritual. We go from seeing in the spirit to looking in the natural.

Seeing Without Looking

Peripheral vision plays a unique role in developing spiritual sight. Unlike direct focus, which engages the natural mind and physical senses, peripheral vision allows us to see in a more relaxed, receptive state. It's almost as if the spiritual eyes are active when we are not consciously trying to use them. This is why so many spiritual glimpses occur when we are not actively "looking" but instead simply observing our surroundings passively.

When we turn our full attention to what we've glimpsed, the shift to physical focus can disrupt the spiritual perception. It's not that what we saw was unreal; it's that our spiritual eyes function on a different level than our physical eyes. To develop spiritual sight, we must learn to engage that peripheral awareness intentionally, training ourselves to discern without relying solely on physical senses.

This concept highlights an important truth: spiritual sight is often more about receiving than striving. It is a posture of openness and sensitivity, rather than intense effort or concentration. By practicing exercises that engage peripheral vision, we can sharpen our spiritual awareness and learn to "see" with clarity and confidence.

Peripheral Vision Exercises

1. The "Spiritual Movement" Exercise

Training yourself to notice spiritual movements or presences in your peripheral vision.

Sit in a quiet, dimly lit room where you won't be disturbed. Relax your body and quiet your mind with a simple prayer, such as, "Lord, open my eyes to see as You see. Help me to perceive what is happening in the spirit."

Focus your physical eyes on a central point in the room— a candle, a piece of furniture, or an empty space. Keep your gaze soft and unfocused, as though you are daydreaming.

Without moving your eyes, become aware of your peripheral vision. Pay attention to the "edges" of your sight. Do you notice any flickers, shadows, or movements? These might be subtle shifts in light or an impression of a presence.

If you sense something, resist the urge to turn and look directly. Instead, remain still and ask the Holy Spirit, "What am I perceiving?" or "Lord, is there something You want to show me?"

After the exercise, write down what you observed or sensed. Over time, you may notice patterns or increased clarity in your perceptions.

2. The "Empty Space Awareness" Exercise

Develop sensitivity to spiritual presences by focusing on "empty" areas of your surroundings.

Find a quiet space where you can sit or stand comfortably. Begin with a brief prayer, inviting God's involvement: "Holy Spirit, I invite You to teach me and open my spiritual eyes."

Select an area of the room—perhaps a corner, an open doorway, or the space above a chair—and focus on it gently. Keep your gaze soft, as though you are looking "through" the space rather than at it.

While keeping your focus on the chosen area, allow your peripheral vision to become active. Notice any impressions, light shifts, or movements around the edges of your sight. Don't be anxious, just let yourself be open to seeing what comes.

If you sense something—a faint glow, a figure, or an impression—ask the Lord for discernment: "Lord, what are You showing me?" or "Is this something I need to know or act on?"

Avoid moving your head or shifting your gaze. The goal is to remain in a state of quiet receptivity, allowing your spiritual perception to sharpen.

After completing the exercise, take time to journal your observations. This practice not only strengthens spiritual sight but also helps you recognize God's presence in ordinary spaces.

3. THE "SPIRITUAL LIGHT DETECTOR" EXERCISE

Train yourself to perceive spiritual light or energy in your surroundings.

Sit in a softly lit room. Position yourself so that you are facing an open area without physical distractions.

Close your eyes for a moment and pray: "Lord, allow me to perceive the light of Your presence. Help me to sense Your glory in the spiritual realm."

Open your eyes and look softly at the space in front of you. Without focusing on a specific object, notice any subtle changes in brightness, faint glows, or colors in your peripheral vision.

As you notice light or movement, remain still and attentive. Avoid trying to analyze or "force" an interpretation. Simply observe and allow the Holy Spirit to reveal meaning. Continue to see without "looking."

Conclude the exercise with thankfulness, thanking God for what He has revealed. Write down any impressions or details to reflect on later.

Peripheral vision is a powerful tool in the development of spiritual sight because it bypasses the analytical, natural mind. By training yourself to engage this type of awareness, you allow your spiritual eyes to perceive without interference from physical senses. Over time, these exercises will help you transition from fleeting glimpses to clearer, more sustained spiritual perception. Remember, spiritual sight is a gift from God, and as you faithfully practice, He will sharpen your vision and increase your understanding of His presence and activity. After a time, this benefit of seeing so naturally and almost accidentally migrates to other ways you see.

CHAPTER FOUR

PERCEIVING LIGHT AND DARKNESS

Discernment in the Spiritual Realm

The spiritual realm often manifests in ways that are subtle but powerful, and light and darkness are two key elements that reveal spiritual dynamics. These are not just physical phenomena; they carry actual, atmospheric power and symbolic meanings that can provide insight into what is happening in the unseen realm.

Throughout Scripture, light symbolizes God's presence, purity, truth, and revelation. Jesus declared, *"I am the light of the world. Whoever follows me will never walk in darkness, but will have the light of life"* (John 8:12). Darkness, on the other hand, often represents confusion, oppression, or the absence of God's presence. Learning to discern shifts in light and darkness can sharpen your spiritual senses, helping you to recognize the presence of God, angelic activity, or even areas where spiritual warfare is taking place.

Understanding Light and Darkness Perception

When we speak of perceiving light and darkness spiritually, it goes beyond what our physical eyes can see. You may notice a literal change in the atmosphere, a brightness that cannot be explained by natural light, or a heaviness that feels like a shadow in the room. This is especially true at night when there is little natural light around you. The sudden brightening of the room makes it very clear that the phenomenon is completely spiritual. These impressions may also come as physical sensations, emotional shifts, or inner awareness rather than visual changes. It should come as no surprise that your physical senses can and do react to spiritual stimuli.

For example, you might walk into a room and sense peace and warmth as though a light has filled the space, even if the lighting is dim. This could indicate God's presence or the prayers of others saturating the atmosphere. Conversely, you might enter a space that feels heavy, unsettling, or even oppressive, which could signify darkness or a spiritual opposition or a lack of God's influence in that environment.

Developing the ability to discern these shifts is not about fear but about awareness. As you grow in this practice, you will become more sensitive to spiritual dynamics and better equipped to respond with prayer, worship, or declarations of the Word of God.

Exercises for Light and Darkness Perception

1. The "Atmospheric Shift" Exercise

Train your spirit to recognize subtle changes in the spiritual atmosphere.

Choose a dimly lit or darkened room where you can sit undisturbed. Begin with a simple prayer, such as, "Lord, open my spiritual senses and help me discern what is happening in this space."

Relax your body and let your physical eyes rest on an "empty" area of the room, such as a blank wall or an open space. Keep your gaze soft and unfocused, allowing your peripheral vision to become active.

Pay attention to any impressions or changes you notice. Does the room feel peaceful, light, and welcoming? Or is there a sense of heaviness, unease, or tension? You may also notice subtle shifts, such as flickers of light, shadows, or movements.

Ask the Holy Spirit for discernment about what you are sensing. If the space feels heavy or dark, pray for God's presence to fill the room, declaring His truth and authority. If it feels light and peaceful, take a moment to worship and thank Him for His presence.

Write down your observations and responses. Over time, you will begin to notice patterns and develop greater confidence in discerning spiritual atmospheres.

2. The "Light Revealed" Exercise

Learn to perceive spiritual light and it's meaning in different environments.

Visit two or three different locations—your home, a church, or an outdoor setting—and repeat this exercise in each space. Begin by asking, "Lord, show me Your light and Your presence in this place."

Sit quietly and observe both your physical surroundings and your spiritual impressions. Do you notice a literal brightness in the atmosphere, even in a dim room? Is there a sense of clarity, openness, or warmth that seems to radiate around you?

Reflect on what the light might mean or represent in this context. Is God highlighting His presence, an area of ministry, or a need for prayer in this space?

Pray or worship based on what you discern. If you sense God's presence, thank Him and ask how He wants to move in that moment. If you perceive a lack of light, pray for His truth and power to penetrate the space. Ask the Lord to fill and overflow the space with His presence.

Why This Matters

Perceiving light and darkness helps us navigate the spiritual realm with sensitivity and clarity. These exercises train us to respond to God's presence and to recognize spiritual realities around us. Whether you sense peace and light or heaviness and darkness, the key is to remain anchored in God's truth, trusting that His light dispels all darkness. As you grow in this practice, you'll find that your spiritual discernment becomes sharper, and your ability to partner with God in the unseen realm becomes more effective and makes a greater impact for the Kingdom.

CHAPTER FIVE

IMAGINATION AS A BRIDGE

The Bridge to Spiritual Perception

The imagination is a profound tool that God has given us—a bridge connecting the natural and spiritual realms. While many see imagination as something reserved for fantasy, pretending or creativity, it holds a much deeper purpose. When we use our imagination intentionally, we activate our spirit's ability to perceive spiritual realities that are otherwise hidden from the natural eye and communicate them to us. Imagination, then, becomes a powerful means of crossing into the spiritual realm, allowing us to "see," "hear," and "experience" what our spirit already knows.

This bridge between realms is something we can strengthen with practice. The more we use our imagination to engage the spiritual, the shorter and easier the "walk" becomes. Eventually, with enough practice, this bridge that once required deliberate effort turns into a simple doorway—one that we can pass through almost effortlessly. Imagination ceases to be a distant "bridge" and instead becomes a doorway that allows us to step from the natural into the spiritual realm with ease.

Imagination is not merely about creating images in our minds; it is a training ground for our spiritual senses. By practicing the art of imaginative engagement, we allow our spirit to inform our conscious mind about the spiritual realities around us. Over time, what was once imaginative visualization becomes an actual spiritual experience, and we find ourselves perceiving the unseen realm naturally.

Training the Imagination for Spiritual Perception

Most people let their imaginations wander freely, allowing them to go wherever they will. But when we desire to engage with the spiritual realm, we are training and focusing our imagination through practice, exercise, and repetition. This intentional training makes imagination a disciplined tool that opens the door to the unseen realm. Just as athletes use visualization to enhance performance, we can use imagination to develop our spiritual awareness. Our focus, however, is not on physical mastery but on spiritual perception.

When we use imagination to envision the spiritual, we are not conjuring something imaginary; instead, we are building a bridge to a reality that already exists. The human mind, when engaged deeply, does not differentiate between a real experience and a vividly imagined one. For example, athletes who imagine performing a routine perfectly can experience measurable improvements, as if they had physically practiced it. Similarly, when we imagine the spiritual realm with focus and intention, our spirit recognizes and interacts with that reality, eventually bridging it into our conscious awareness.

How Imagination Builds an Openness to the Spiritual Realm

Engaging with the spiritual through imagination also builds a kind of faith. When we imagine supernatural experiences—such as seeing an angel or hearing God's voice—we give ourselves permission to believe that these things are real and accessible. Each time we visualize such an encounter, we strengthen our readiness to receive these experiences, making us more open to spiritual reality.

Imagine, for example, that I ask you to point to where an angel is standing in the room. Even without the benefit of spiritual sight, you might use your imagination to "see" the angel, picturing his appearance, his position, and even his expression. You're not only practicing spiritual seeing but also training your awareness of what it feels like to perceive angelic presence. This exercise familiarizes your mind with the sensation of seeing in the spirit, making it more natural over time.

But there's another layer: your spirit already sees. Even if your conscious mind doesn't recognize it, your spirit knows where the angel is and is aware of his presence fully. Often, when we imagine where an angel is or how he appears, we "guess" based on what our spirit is subtly communicating to us. Our imagination becomes a bridge through which our spirit informs our conscious awareness, allowing us to recognize and respond to the spiritual world.

The more we practice seeing, hearing, and feeling through imagination, the more these experiences become real. After visualizing the spiritual realm a thousand times, you reach a point where you don't even need to "try"—it simply happens. You've trained your spiritual senses through the doorway of imagination, and now you can "see" and "hear" as naturally as you would in the physical realm.

Imagination as a Powerful Spiritual Tool

Imagination is more than a mental exercise; it's a powerful spiritual force that can shape our perception of the unseen realm. By using it regularly, especially in the beginning stages of developing spiritual sight, we create a solid foundation for natural spiritual experiences. The following benefits highlight why imagination is such a crucial tool in building spiritual perception:

Familiarity with Spiritual Sensations:

Imagination helps us become familiar with what it "feels" like to perceive in the spirit. By picturing scenes, images, or spiritual beings, we're creating a familiarity that lowers mental and spiritual barriers to actual perception.

Strengthening Focus and Clarity:

One of the challenges with imagination is maintaining sharp focus. At first, it may feel difficult to hold onto images or sensations without distraction. Details become "muddy" and hard to maintain for extended periods of time. But as we practice, our ability to focus becomes stronger, and the images or impressions become clearer. Eventually, these sensations integrate with our spiritual sight, allowing us to see clearly and confidently.

Accelerating Spiritual Sensitivity

Each time we use imagination with a holy or spiritual intent, we're accelerating the development of our spiritual senses. Conversely, if we use our imagination for wrong purposes it is like putting mud in our eyes, making it more difficult to see. But as we practice in the right way we're giving our mind permission to accept what the spirit already perceives, which bridges the gap between knowing and seeing. As we persist, and practice, imagination turns into direct perception, and we find ourselves stepping naturally into the spiritual realm.

IMAGINATION-BASED SPIRITUAL EXERCISES

Let's take a closer look at how imagination-based exercises open our spiritual senses and lead us to genuine spiritual encounters. Here's a step-by-step example of an exercise in which you might use imagination to perceive an angel's presence in the room:

Sit in a quiet place, close your eyes, and ask God to help you see with the eyes of your spirit. Calm your mind and set an intention to see the angelic presence in the room, inviting the Lord to guide your perception.

Engage Your Imagination:

Begin by imagining where the angel might be standing. Picture his figure, his light, or any details that come to mind. Allow yourself to visualize his position, his posture, and even his expression. Don't rush the process and don't force it; simply let your imagination create the image naturally.

Tune into Spiritual Impressions:

As you imagine the angel, pay attention to any subtle impressions in your spirit. You may notice a feeling of peace or a sense of warmth in a specific part of the room.

Trust these impressions, even if they feel faint or uncertain. Often, your spirit is guiding you, revealing spiritual realities that your imagination is helping you perceive.

Reflect on the Experience:

When you finish, take a moment to reflect on the experience. Was there a particular place in the room where the presence felt stronger? Did you sense anything that seemed beyond your imagination alone? These reflections help reinforce your awareness and build confidence in your growing spiritual sight.

IMAGINATION-BASED SPIRITUAL SEEING

Using imagination to engage the spiritual realm may feel challenging at first, but with practice, it becomes second nature. What we are contending for is first nature. I say this because we are spiritual beings. Each time we visualize and "see" spiritually, we train our spirit to cross the bridge between the natural and spiritual realms. Eventually, as I have mentioned previously, this bridge turns into a doorway, and stepping into the spiritual realm becomes as effortless as passing from one room to another.

Through consistent use, imagination becomes a powerful spiritual tool, enabling us to see and perceive the unseen realm. This process builds faith, strengthens focus, and familiarizes us with spiritual perception. Over time, imagination-based exercises are no longer just training—they become real, tangible encounters with God's presence and activity. The exercise becomes lifestyle. By embracing imagination as a bridge, we allow our spirit to lead us naturally and confidently into the realm of the unseen, transforming imagination into revelation.

EXERCISE:
ENVISIONING HEAVEN'S REFINING FIRE

Developing Spiritual Sight and Receiving Transformation

This exercise invites you to use your imagination as a bridge to the spiritual realm, combining the development of spiritual sight with an opportunity to receive from God what you deeply need—cleansing, love, compassion, strength, or holiness. By immersing yourself in scripture, imagining the scene, and engaging all your senses, you are practicing the art of seeing in the Spirit and opening your heart and being for spiritual transformation.

Begin in a place of stillness, free from interruptions. Quiet your mind and prepare your heart to focus completely on this exercise. Have your Bible open to Isaiah 6:1-8, where the prophet Isaiah recounts his vision of Heaven.

Read the passage slowly and prayerfully, allowing its imagery to unfold in your mind: Read it several times if you need to, to create a vivid image in your mind.

"In the year that King Uzziah died, I saw the Lord, high and exalted, seated on a throne; and the train of His robe filled the temple. Above Him were seraphim,

each with six wings: With two wings they covered their faces, with two they covered their feet, and with two they were flying. And they were calling to one another: 'Holy, holy, holy is the Lord Almighty; the whole earth is full of His glory.'"

Take time to absorb the description—the grandeur, the majesty, and the overwhelming holiness of God. Imagine the sounds of the seraphim calling out, the brilliance of the light filling the temple, and the awe of being in the presence of the Most High.

Entering the Scene

Close your eyes and imagine yourself standing beside Isaiah as he beholds this incredible vision. Feel the weight of the atmosphere—the overwhelming sense of holiness, the electric energy in the air, and the reverberation of the seraphim's voices echoing, "Holy, holy, holy."

Pay attention to every detail: the radiant light, the shimmering movement of the seraphim, the fragrance of the altar, and the heaviness of the glory filling the temple. Use your imagination to experience this scene fully, as though you are truly present.

Now, see Isaiah fall to his knees, confessing, *"Woe to me! I am ruined! For I am a man of unclean lips, and I live among a people of unclean lips, and my eyes have seen the King, the Lord Almighty."* Sense his humility and awe. As you stand beside him, reflect on your own life. What areas do you long for God to refine? What impurities or weaknesses do you want to bring before Him?

Receiving the Refining Touch

Now, imagine the seraph as it takes a glowing coal from the altar and approaches Isaiah. See the moment of transformation as the coal touches his lips, removing his guilt and sin. Imagine another seraph turning to you, carrying a similar coal. See it draw near and touch your lips, hear its voice declaring, *"Your guilt is taken away, and your sin atoned for."*

Feel the reality of this moment—God's holiness cleansing and refining you. Let this imagined experience become a prayer of your heart, asking God to purify and prepare you, just as He did Isaiah.

Repeat this exercise often, allowing more details to emerge and your imagination to deepen. Over time, you'll notice how your spiritual senses sharpen, making the experience more vivid than natural reality. As you practice, trust that God honors the intent of your heart and works through these moments to bring genuine transformation. Expect the arrival of the Seraphim!

AN ALTERNATE PASSAGE: EZEKIEL'S VISION

For another example, consider Ezekiel's vision of the valley of dry bones in Ezekiel 37:1-10. In this vision, Ezekiel is led by the Spirit into a valley filled with dry bones, and God asks him to prophesy over them so they might live. Imagine yourself standing with Ezekiel, seeing the bones scattered across the valley, feeling the weight of despair in the scene. Hear Ezekiel's voice declare the Word of the Lord and watch as the bones come together, flesh appears, and breath enters them, bringing them to life.

As you visualize this, reflect on areas in your life that feel lifeless or broken. See God breathing new life into those areas, renewing hope, and restoring strength. Again, make this a prayer as you imagine it, trusting God to bring His Word to life in you.

ENCOURAGEMENT AND PRACTICE

Your imagination might seem scattered or faint, but don't be discouraged. Like any spiritual discipline, this practice strengthens with repetition. The imagination is a powerful God-given tool to help us move into spiritual reality. As you practice, this becomes a proficiency that allows us to move more easily into divine encounters.

God sees the desires of your heart and honors your intention to draw closer to Him. These exercises are not merely imaginative—they are prayers in motion, acts of faith that invite God's presence and refining power. Trust Him to meet you in these moments, to sharpen your spiritual sight, and to transform your life in ways you cannot yet imagine.

Imagination Exercises

Here are some additional imagination-based exercises for developing spiritual sight and deepening your connection with the spiritual realm. These exercises are faith-driven, rooted in Christian principles, and designed to help you engage with God, His Word, and the unseen reality He has revealed.

1. Walking with Jesus

Strengthen your relationship with Christ and learn to "see" Him in your everyday life.

Find a quiet place to sit or lie down. Close your eyes and imagine yourself in a peaceful setting—perhaps a garden, a quiet path, or by a lake.

Picture Jesus walking toward you. Visualize His face, His clothing, and His presence. Imagine how it feels to be near Him—peace, love, acceptance.

Walk alongside Him, talking with Him about your concerns, questions, or joys. Pause and "listen" for His responses. This may come as impressions, feelings, or words in your mind.

End by thanking Him for His presence and reflecting on what you experienced.

2. The Throne Room

Build reverence for God and spiritual awareness.

Read Revelation 4 to familiarize yourself with the imagery of the throne room.

Close your eyes and visualize entering the throne room of God. See the throne, the One seated upon it, and the emerald rainbow encircling it.

Hear the voices of angels and the sound of worship as they cry, "Holy, holy, holy is the Lord God Almighty."

Imagine yourself bowing before God, offering Him your worship and presenting any burdens you carry.

Reflect on the majesty of God and ask Him to give you insight or direction for your life.

3. Armor of God

Activate spiritual protection and awareness of God's provision.

Meditate on Ephesians 6:10-18, where Paul describes the armor of God.

Imagine yourself putting on each piece of the armor. As you "put on" the helmet of salvation, the breastplate of righteousness, the belt of truth, etc., visualize its appearance and feel its weight and fit.

As you equip yourself, think about what each piece represents and pray for God's strength and protection in those areas of your life.

Picture yourself standing firm in the armor, ready to face spiritual challenges with confidence.

4. CROSSING THE JORDAN

Practice stepping into new levels of faith and spiritual boldness.

Read Joshua 3, where the Israelites cross the Jordan River into the Promised Land.

Imagine standing on the riverbank, with the water flowing rapidly before you. Feel the anticipation and fear of stepping into the unknown.

Visualize the priests carrying the Ark of the Covenant stepping into the water and the river parting. Imagine yourself following behind them, stepping onto dry ground.

Reflect on areas in your life where you need to trust God for breakthrough and victory. Pray for courage and take time to "see" yourself stepping forward in faith.

5. HEALING BY THE POOL

Experience God's healing power emotionally, physically, or spiritually.

Read John 5:1-9, the story of the man at the pool of Bethesda.

Close your eyes and place yourself at the edge of the pool. Imagine the water stirring and feel the expectancy of healing in the air.

See Jesus approaching you. Hear Him ask, "Do you want to be made well?"

Imagine Jesus speaking healing over you, or physically touching the area of your life that needs restoration.

Visualize His love and power bringing wholeness to your body, mind, or spirit.

6. GATHERING MANNA

Practice reliance on God for daily provision.

Reflect on Exodus 16, where God provides manna for the Israelites.

Picture yourself in the wilderness as the morning dew evaporates and the ground is covered with manna.

Kneel down and gather the bread of heaven, symbolizing God's provision. Imagine its texture, smell, and taste as you partake.

Thank God for meeting your needs and reflect on the areas where you need to trust Him more fully.

7. STANDING IN THE GAP

Intercede for others while growing in spiritual sensitivity.

Visualize yourself standing in a gap, like a bridge between two cliffs. On one side is the person or situation you're praying for; on the other side is God's presence.

Imagine yourself lifting that person or situation up in prayer, placing them in God's hands.

Picture God responding with light, grace, or healing flowing from His presence into the situation.

Reflect on the peace and assurance that God is at work.

8. DRINKING FROM THE FOUNTAIN OF LIFE

Receive spiritual refreshment and renewal.

Meditate on Revelation 22:1-2, which describes the river of life flowing from the throne of God.

Imagine kneeling beside this river. Hear the sound of the water and feel it's refreshing presence.

See yourself dipping a cup or your hands into the water and drinking deeply. Imagine the renewal and strength it brings to your spirit.

Reflect on God's promise of eternal life and His sustaining presence.

How Imagination Bridges to Reality

Imagination is in fact reality. Jesus said *"But I say to you that whoever looks at a woman to lust for her has already committed adultery with her in his heart"* (Matthew 5:28). Notice that Jesus did not say "they have pretended to commit adultery" or "They imagined committing adultery." He said they have committed adultery in their heart. The reason imagination is so powerful in accessing the spiritual realm is because it is real. And it allows us to engage with truths that are not immediately visible, making unseen realities tangible and accessible. Here are some connections imagination makes for Believers.

1. Imagination Aligns Us with Faith

Faith and imagination are closely linked. Faith itself is the substance of things hoped for and the evidence of things not seen (Hebrews 11:1). Imagination provides the mind's canvas to visualize what faith apprehends in the spiritual realm. By imagining biblical truths—God's promises, His presence, or spiritual realities—we align our thoughts and emotions with what we believe, bringing those truths closer to our conscious awareness.

For example, when we imagine the throne room of God or visualize Jesus standing beside us, we are engaging with spiritual truths. Though unseen by physical eyes, these are no less real. Imagination helps us to focus on these realities, deepening our faith and making them more present in our lives.

2. Imagination Trains the Mind to Perceive the Spirit

Imagination is a form of meditation. When we focus our thoughts on a particular truth or scene—like Jesus calming the storm or Isaiah's encounter in the throne room—we are training our minds to recognize and engage with spiritual realities. This practice builds sensitivity to the Spirit and opens the door for spiritual encounters.

For example, imagining Jesus' compassion for others as recorded in the Gospels can help us develop a heart of compassion in reality. (What we focus on we connect with) The exercise shapes our character and transforms our inner world, enabling us to live out what we meditate on.

3. Imagination Prepares Us for Spiritual Experiences

In the spiritual realm, practice often precedes experience. Just as athletes visualize their performance to prepare their bodies and minds, using imagination in prayer or meditation primes us for genuine spiritual encounters.

For instance, when we imagine hearing God's voice during stillness, we are training ourselves to recognize His voice when it comes. This practice helps to bridge the gap for us between an imagined reality and an actual experience. The imagined has the capability of becoming real.

4. God Honors the Intent of Our Hearts

When we use imagination in pursuit of spiritual truths, God responds to the desires and intents of our hearts. As we imagine standing before God or walking with Jesus, we are praying with our minds and engaging with Him on a spiritual level. While the act may begin as imaginative, it invites real interaction with God.

For example, many believers who engage in imaginative prayer report moments when what they are visualizing becomes unexpectedly vivid or profound. These moments are often accompanied by a sense of God's presence, signaling a transition from imagination to spiritual reality. We also know that God can hear and respond to prayers we pray in our mind. People are often in situations where it is impossible to pray aloud so they pray in their imagination.

5. Imagination Builds Expectation and Spiritual Awareness

The imagination also sets our expectations. When we visualize and focus on God's promises—such as His healing power, provision, or presence—we condition our minds and spirits to look for and recognize these realities in our lives. This heightened awareness makes us more aware of how God is moving.

For example, if you imagine the peace of Jesus calming the storm, you may find yourself more aware of His peace in a moment of personal turmoil. The imagined experience becomes a framework for recognizing His reality in your life. We build a sound foundation that has real power in our lives.

6. Imagination Engages All Our Senses

Imagination bridges to reality by engaging multiple senses, making spiritual truths more tangible. When you visualize yourself in a biblical scene or imagine standing in God's presence, you can incorporate sights, sounds, smells, and even feelings. This multisensory engagement deepens the experience, anchoring it more firmly in your mind and spirit.

For example, imagining the fragrance of the incense in Heaven or the warmth of God's light can make your time in prayer or meditation feel as real as a physical experience. Having said that, I firmly believe the spiritual experience is the greater experience. The seen was created from the unseen.

7. The Bible Models Imaginative Practices

Scripture often invites us to visualize and meditate on its truths. Jesus frequently used parables and vivid imagery to communicate spiritual realities, engaging His listeners' imaginations to convey truths about the Kingdom of God. In the same way, prophets like Ezekiel, Isaiah, and John experienced visions that engaged their senses and imaginations, providing a bridge between what was seen in the spirit and understood in reality.

When we imagine, we are following biblical patterns of engaging with the unseen to apprehend spiritual truths.

8. Imagination Cultivates Spiritual Boldness

When we consistently engage in imaginative exercises rooted in scripture, we become more confident in stepping into spiritual realities. The bridge of imagination builds familiarity and faith, reducing fear and uncertainty. Over time, what begins as imaginative prayer becomes a natural and real interaction with God.

For example, visualizing yourself laying down burdens at the feet of Jesus can lead to the real experience of feeling lighter, freer, and more at peace.

CHAPTER SIX

SPIRITUAL HEARING

Here are several exercises for developing spiritual hearing—the ability to perceive and discern God's voice, messages, and guidance through spiritual means. These exercises are rooted in biblical principles and are designed to sharpen your sensitivity to what God is saying.

1. LISTENING IN STILLNESS

Cultivate an increased awareness of God's voice in a quiet environment.

Find a quiet place where you won't be interrupted. Sit comfortably and close your eyes.

Pray a simple prayer, such as, "Lord, I am here to listen to You. Speak to me in any way You choose."

Spend several minutes in silence. Focus on the Lord, inviting the Holy Spirit to calm your mind.

Pay attention to any impressions, thoughts, or scriptures that come to mind. Write them down, even if they seem small or unrelated. Over time, you'll begin to recognize patterns in how God speaks to you.

2. SCRIPTURE WHISPERING

Use scripture as a channel to tune into God's voice.

Choose a short verse, such as Psalm 46:10: "Be still, and know that I am God."

Whisper the verse aloud slowly and repeatedly, focusing on the words. Let them resonate in your mind and spirit.

As you repeat the verse, listen for any additional insights, phrases, or directions that may arise in your spirit. Write these down and reflect on them.

As the Lord Jesus once told me, *"Every time you speaks something changes."*

3. INNER DIALOGUE WITH GOD

Develop the ability to discern God's voice in your thoughts.

Begin by talking with God in your heart as if having a conversation with a trusted friend. Share your concerns, questions, or praises.

After sharing, pause and listen internally. What thoughts or impressions come to mind?

Test these impressions against scripture. God's voice will always align with His Word and reflect His character.

Practice this regularly to become more familiar with God's voice in your inner dialogue.

4. ATMOSPHERIC LISTENING

Discern the spiritual "tone" or presence in a room or situation.

Enter a room or environment and pause. Pray silently, asking God to help you perceive what is happening spiritually in that space.

Pay attention to the "atmosphere." Does it feel peaceful, joyful, heavy, or unsettling?

Ask God for discernment about what you're sensing and how to respond. This practice helps you become attuned to spiritual dynamics around you.

5. GUIDED IMAGINATION: HEARING JESUS

Use your imagination to engage with Jesus and develop spiritual hearing.

Close your eyes and imagine sitting with Jesus in a peaceful setting, such as a garden or by a lake. Picture Him clearly—His expression, His movements.

Imagine Jesus speaking to you. What does He say? How does His voice sound? Listen closely and write down what you hear.

Reflect on the words, sounds and impressions, testing them against scripture to ensure they align with God's truth.

6. WRITING THE WHISPER

Practice journaling what you sense God is saying.

Begin your prayer time by asking, "Lord, what do You want to say to me today?"

Sit quietly and listen. As thoughts or impressions come, write them down without overanalyzing.

Review what you've written. Does it align with scripture? Does it bring peace, conviction, or encouragement? Over time, this practice helps you discern God's voice from your own thoughts.

7. NOTICING REPETITION

Recognize patterns in how God speaks.

Pay attention to repeated themes, words, or scriptures that arise during prayer, conversations, or sermons. God has a way of speaking to each person differently. He has a personal connection with you.

Write these down in a notebook or journal. Often and according to scripture, repetition is a way in which God emphasizes something important.

Pray for clarity, asking God what He is saying through these repeated messages.

8. SINGING AND WORSHIP LISTENING

Hear God's voice in worship.

Spend time worshiping through music. Sing songs that focus on God's greatness and love.

After a few songs, pause and ask, "Lord, is there anything You want to speak to me during this time?"

Very often, especially in stillness at night an atmosphere is established than is tangible.

Listen for any impressions, scriptures, or ideas that arise. This exercise creates space for God to speak during your worship.

9. Practicing Obedience

Strengthen your ability to recognize and act on God's voice and direction.

Throughout your day, ask God for small prompts: "Lord, what would You like me to do right now?"

Listen for a subtle nudge or thought, such as calling someone, praying for someone, or making a specific choice.

Test these prompts with scripture and God's character, then act on them. Over time, this practice helps you distinguish His voice from other influences.

The Bible says "We have not because we ask not"(James 4:3) In all of the exercises we are continually engaging with God, asking His help and accepting His direction. We want the Holy Spirit to be the one leading this endeavor in every way. I have found that most of the time I don't even know what questions to ask. Let Him lead you.

10. Group Listening

Practice hearing God as a group for confirmation and encouragement.

Gather with a few trusted believers. Spend time in prayer and ask a specific question, such as, "Lord, what do You want to say about [topic]?"

Each person listens silently for a few minutes and writes down what they sense.

Share your impressions with the group. Often, God will give complementary or confirming insights, helping you recognize His voice more clearly. The great thing about this is it is an opportunity to bond with other believers and sharpen each other. Oftentimes we can feel very much alone in this journey. Doint activations and exercises as a group is a great way to be encouraged.

11. Listening to Nature

Hear God's voice through His creation.

Spend time outdoors in a quiet, natural setting. Observe the beauty around you and reflect on God as the Creator.

Ask God to speak to you through what you see, hear, or feel in nature. This may sound a bit strange but nature does speak, we just need to learn to hear it.

Psalm 19:1-4 (NIV)

"The heavens declare the glory of God; the skies proclaim the work of His hands. Day after day they pour forth speech; night after night they reveal knowledge. They have no speech, they use no words; no

sound is heard from them. Yet their voice goes out into all the earth, their words to the ends of the world." (Psalm 19:1-4 NIV)

Job 12:7-9 (NIV)

"But ask the animals, and they will teach you, or the birds in the sky, and they will tell you; or speak to the earth, and it will teach you, or let the fish in the sea inform you. Which of all these does not know that the hand of the Lord has done this?" (Job 12:7-9 NIV)

"I tell you," He replied, "if they keep quiet, the stones will cry out." (Luke 19:40 NIV)

Nature speaks, write down any impressions or insights that arise during your time outside.

12. ASKING SPECIFIC QUESTIONS

Focus your listening by presenting specific concerns to God.

Ask the Lord a direct question, such as, "Lord, what do You want me to know about this decision?" or "How do You see me?"

Sit quietly and listen for a response. Be patient, as answers may come as impressions, scriptures, or subtle thoughts.

Remember that His answers will line up with His Word.

Record your experience and reflect on it later.

Encouragement for Practice

Hearing God's voice is a skill that develops over time. At first, it may feel like your own thoughts, but with practice, you'll begin to distinguish His voice. It is very similar to any relationship in the natural. The more you hear someone's voice the more you recognize it. Be patient, stay rooted in scripture, and trust the Holy Spirit to guide you. God desires to speak to His children, and as you seek Him, you'll grow in confidence and clarity in hearing His voice.

CONCLUSION: IT'S ABOUT DOING

This journey is not just about reading, knowing, or even trying—it's about doing. Spiritual growth and activation happen when we take what we've learned, what we've imagined, and what we've hoped for, and put it into action. Each exercise in this book is designed to guide you into deeper waters, but it is your willingness to step out, engage, and persevere that will bring the breakthrough you desire.

You can do this. You are not alone in this journey. The Holy Spirit is your teacher, your guide, and your empowerer. He walks with you every step of the way, giving you the wisdom and strength to explore the spiritual realm safely and effectively. When you approach these practices with faith and expectancy, you align yourself with God's purposes and open the door for Him to do extraordinary things in your life.

God desires your success. He longs for you to experience the fullness of life He has planned for you—a life of intimacy with Him, power in His Spirit, and purpose in His kingdom. These exercises are not about striving but about positioning yourself to receive. They are a way to create space in your life for God to move, to speak, and to transform you into the person He has called you to be.

Remember, every step of obedience, no matter how small, matters. Every time that you engage with these activations, you are strengthening your spiritual senses, deepening your connection with God, and growing into the fullness of your calling. You don't have to be perfect. You just have to be willing.

So, take the first step. Begin with one exercise, and commit to doing it with your whole heart. Trust that God will meet you there, leading you from strength to strength and glory to glory. The journey may not always be easy, but it will be worth it. You were made for this.

Keep pressing forward, keep trusting Him, and keep doing the work. Breakthrough is not a matter of if—it's a matter of when. God is faithful, and He will complete the work He has begun in you.

Let's step boldly into the fullness of His promises together. Your best days are ahead.

About the Author

Michael Van Vlymen is a writer and speaker who teaches about the supernatural things of God. Michael and his wife Gordana serve the Lord from their home base in Carmel, Indiana USA.

Others Books by this Author

How to See in the Spirit

Powerful Keys to Spiritual Sight

Waiting on God

Made in the USA
Columbia, SC
04 February 2025

53280178R00050